to:

. . . . ⭐

from:

. . . .

date:

. . . .

Little Prayers
to Bless Your Day

Illustrations and text by Chris Shea

HARVEST HOUSE PUBLISHERS

EUGENE, OREGON

Little Prayers to Bless Your Day

Copyright © 2012 by Chris Shea
Lifesighs Cards, PO Box 19446, San Diego, CA 92159

Published by Harvest House Publishers
Eugene, Oregon 97402
www.harvesthousepublishers.com

ISBN 978-0-7369-4767-1

Design and production by Blum Graphic Design, Wheaton, Illinois

All Scripture quotations are from the King James Version of the Bible.

Printed in China

12 13 14 15 16 17 18 / LP / 10 9 8 7 6 5 4 3 2 1

For Ethel Young

Thank you
for the light you shine.

Dear God,
I've been thinking about
all the prayers

I have said throughout my life...

prayers in church
surrounded by people I love,

prayers before I take

even one bite of food,

prayers beside my child's bed,

prayers in a hospital room

for someone dear to me,

or prayers as I fall asleep

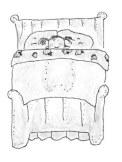

at the end of a busy day.

What a gift, prayer!

What if I used this gift oftener?

What if I prayed when I wasn't
in church or at the table,
at the hospital or falling asleep?

What if I prayed
in between those times?

What if I prayed just as I got out of bed
or while I was at the grocery store?

What if I listened more carefully
for the opportunity to pray
throughout my day;

little prayers would bless me
and those I care about, wouldn't they?

Maybe I'll start tomorrow
with a little prayer
as soon as I get out of bed.

Amen.

Prayer for Getting Out of Bed

Bless my feet
and the floor I put them on.
Bless the rug
that warms my toes.
Help me walk today in the right direction
toward the infinite opportunities
that spread out along
my pathway today . . .
and every day.

   Amen.

The day is thine.

Psalm 74:16

A Little Prayer for the Grocery Store

May I never grumble
about having to go to the store.
Such bounty to behold—
a blessing many do not have.
May the sight of
a fresh bunch of carrots
and a cold bottle of milk
never fail to remind me
how truly rich I am.

Amen.

My heart is glad.

Psalm 16:9

Prayer for Dogs

Thank You for the incomparable gift!
You've lent us dogs, loyalty and trust
and unconditional love wrapped in fur
with wagging tails!
Help all of us, blessed by their presence,
to provide them with a home
that feels like heaven on earth.
That way, when we have to give them back,
they'll still feel right at home.

Amen.

O LORD, thou preservest man and beast.
Psalm 36:6

Prayer for Cats

Dear Lord,
Thank You for the cat, a daily reminder
of strength and grace and wisdom.
Just by being, cats remind us
that an afternoon nap in the sunshine
is bliss.
Thank You also for the soothing sound
of their purr, a heavenly sound if ever
there was one.

Amen.

...Purrr...

The LORD will command his
lovingkindness in the daytime.
Psalm 42:8

Prayer for Washing Dishes

Help me never to forget,
not for one single moment,
how blessed I am to have hot water.
And a kitchen.
May I ever be mindful that a dishpan
nightly filled with dirty dishes
is evidence that I have more food
than some people ever will.
Thank You, Lord, for dishes to wash.

Amen.

My cup runneth over.

Psalm 23:5

A Prayer for Doing Laundry

Dear Lord,
Bless me as I put my clothes
into the washing machine.
And bless me also, if You would,
by reminding me to wash an extra load
of things I never wear anymore
so I can give them to someone who will.

   Amen.

Let us not love in word . . . but in deed.

1 John 3:18

A Prayer for Shoe Shopping

Thank You for my feet that take me
anywhere I want to go.
Bless the people who made the shoes
I am about to try on.
And if I do bring home brand new shoes,
may I make room for them in my closet
by taking a pair
I seldom wear and making sure
they find a new pair of feet to fill them.

   Amen.

Lead me in a plain path.

Psalm 27:11

Prayer Before Getting Angry

Bless my mouth, dear God.
Help me keep it closed until I know
the right thing to say.
I know it's all right if I am angry,
but it's another thing altogether
to lash out at someone.
Even myself.

Amen.

Let me never be ashamed.

Psalm 31:1

A Prayer During Dark Times

Dear God,
Please help me.
I'm feeling pretty discouraged,
but I know
You are there.
Thank You in advance. . .

Amen.

I know that thou canst do every thing.

Job 42:2

A Little Prayer of Gratitude
When Dark Times End

Dear God,
I'm so glad there is You.
What would I do without You?

Amen.

I will not leave you comfortless.

John 14:18

A Prayer for Worrisome Times

Fill my thought with You,
dear Lord.
Please fill it so full
of the knowledge of You
that there is not even
one tiny space
for worry to grow or thrive in.

Amen.

Blessed are all they
that put their trust in him.

Psalm 2:12

A Prayer for Success

Dear God,
I know the world has its own definition
of success.
But I long to have the kind of success
that Jesus had,
the kind of success
that comes from knowing You.
Thank You for Your presence in
every single endeavor of my life.

Amen.

Behold what manner of love
the Father hath bestowed upon us.
1 John 3:1

Prayer Before Complaining

Bless me with Your wisdom.
Help me keep my lips closed
until I make sure
I really, really
want to complain
(or even have a reason to).

Amen.

Be still.

Psalm 4:4

Prayer for Gardening

Bless my trowel and my rake,
my packet of seeds and these knees
I kneel upon.
Never let me forget as I pull weeds
and tend the things You create,
what an honor it is
to touch this precious earth
You made.

Amen.

And the earth brought forth grass . . .
and God saw that it was good.

Genesis 1:12

A Prayer for Neighbors

Dear God,
Thank You for lights that
shine across the street,
for visits over backyard fences,
for borrowed cups of sugar,
and the sounds of kids at play.
Thank You most for those
special moments when a kind "Hello!"
becomes a "Come on in!"

Amen.

Better is a neighbor that is near.
Proverbs 27:10

Prayer for Moments of Impatience

Dear God, please shield the one
I am about to speak unkindly to,
the one who does not deserve
my impatience.
Remind me how patient
You are with me. Remind me that
You are incapable of impatience
and that I, created in Your image,
ought to strive to be the same.

Amen.

Wait, I say, on the LORD.

Psalm 27:14

Prayer for Taking a Walk

Bless the earth I walk upon.
Bless the trees that I walk past
and the sky I walk beneath.
And bless,
please bless, every person I pass by.

Amen.

Lift them up forever.

Psalm 28:9

Prayer for Waiting in Line

Dear God,
May I use this time in line
to look around and see
who might need a silent prayer
of hope or peace or comfort today.
May I be a light in this line,
even just a tiny one,
for someone who needs
just such a blessing.

Amen.

Thou wilt light my candle.

Psalm 18:28

Prayer While Sitting

Dear Lord,
Thank You for this gift of time to sit.
May I be mindful of those
who would love to sit
but instead stand on feet
that are tired.
Thank You for the time to pause
in this place in my day
and ask Your blessing on the world.

Amen.

For he satisfieth the longing soul.

Psalm 107:9

A Little Prayer for Every Day

Dear God,
Thank You.
Thank You.
Thank You.
  Love
  and
  Amen.

Thy lovingkindness is before mine eyes.
Psalm 26:3